قصة الأرقام

THE NUMBER STORY

SMALL BOOK ONE

ENGLISH - ARABIC

Numbers Teach Children Their Number Names

written and illustrated by

MISS ANNA

Early Reader Edition of *The Number Story 1*
Bronze Medal Winner, 2016 Wishing Shelf Book Award

Cover by | Lumpy Publishing
Layout by | Lumpy Publishing
Translated by Ahmad Abouelmagd أحمد أبوالمجد
Coloring by Jieeun Woo and Maria Mirabella

Library of Congress Control Number: 2018902040

Names: Miss Anna, author.
Title: Number story : numbers teach children their number names / Miss Anna.
Description: Portland, OR: Lumpy Publishing, 2018.
Identifiers: ISBN 978-1-945977-40-4| LCCN 2018902040
Summary: The pictures and rhymes present stories which introduce numbers 0-10.
Subjects: LCSH Numeration—English--Arabic--Pictorial works--Juvenile literature. | BISAC JUVENILE NONFICTION /
Languages: English--Arabic
Classification: LCC QA141.3 .M57 2018 | DDC 513—dc23

Publisher: Lumpy Publishing
Website: www.missannabooks.com
Email: missanna@missannabooks.com

Paperback: ISBN 978-1-945977-40-4
Printed in the U.S.A.   1 3 5 7 9 10 8 6 4 2

هل تريد معرفة أسماء الأرقام لدينا؟

It is very easy and a lot of fun!

هذا سهل جداً وبه كثير من المرح.

Say-along our little jingle

تغنى معنا قصتنا الصغيرة.

starting from Number One!

هيا بنا نبدأ من رقم واحد!

ONE   looks like my one finger.

١ واحد

واحد يبدو مثل إصبعي الواحد.

ONE!
واحد !

2

TWO   trails a tail.

٢ اثنين

اثنان مثل مسارين ذيل.

A TAIL! ذيل!

THREE   has bumps.

٣ ثلاثة

ثلاثة لديه مطبات.

انظر إلى التل الأخضر!

4

FOUR carries a sail.

٤ أربعة

أربعة يحمل شراع.

A SAIL!
شراع!
قارب لديه شراع!

5

FIVE is a racing track.

خمسة

خمسة مسار السباق.

VROOM
فرووو؟!

6

SIX curves like a snail.

٦ ستة

ستة ينحني مثل الحلزون.

A SNAIL! ‏الحلزون!‏

7

SEVEN has a sharp angle.

٧ سبعة

سبعة لديه زاوية حادة.

BE CAREFUL! IT'S SHARP!
كن حذراً! أ إنه حاد!

EIGHT is rollercoaster rails.

٨ ثمانية

ثمانية تبدو كمسار السفينة الدوارة.

قطار دوار! ركوب القطار بالدوار.

يبيي !
YIPPEE!

9

NINE is a bubble on a stick.

٩ تسعة

تسعة فقاعة على عصا.

A BUBBLE! فقاعة!

10

TEN is an eye of a whale.

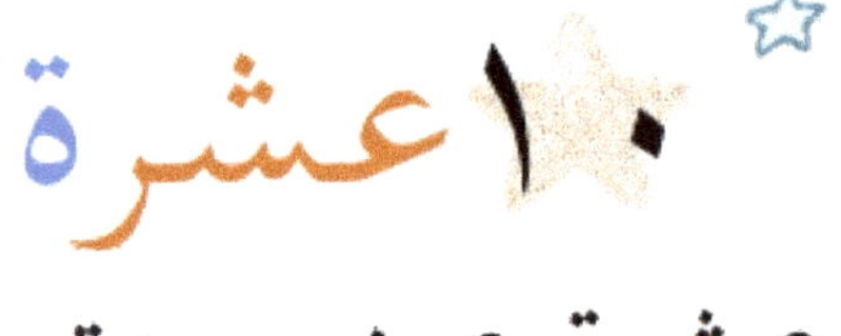

عشرة عين حوت واحدة.

WINK!
غمزة!

HELLO! مرحباً!

And

و

O

ZERO   is an empty pail.

صفر

صفر يبدو مثل الدلو الفارغ.

IT'S EMPTY!
إنه فارغ!

Thank you for playing with us today.

We had a lot of fun too!

شكرا لأنك لعبت معنا اليوم.
كان لدينا الكثير من المرح أيضا!

We are your Number friends,
Zero to Ten,
Who will be here for you~

نحن أصدقائك
من صفر إلى عشرة.
سنكون دائماً هنا من أجلك!

Bye-bye now!
See you again soon!

وداعا الآن!
نراك مرة أخرى قريباً!

The Numbers are *SINGING* too!

To sing-a-long, look for Miss Anna Number Story
at your favorite music store like iTUNES.

MP3

Numbers 0-10
IDENTIFYING
& COUNTING

Numbers 11-20
& Ordinals
first, second, third…

Numbers 0-100
& Place Values
ones, tens, hundreds…

About Clocks
& Telling Time
hours, minutes, seconds

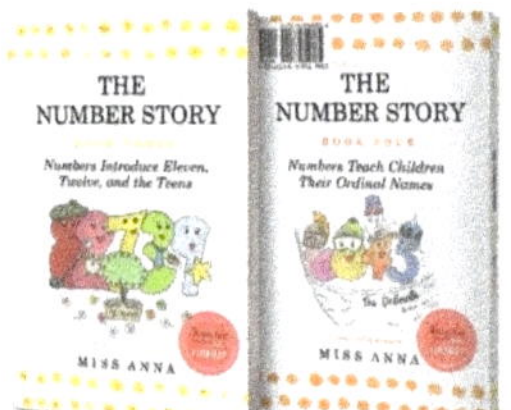

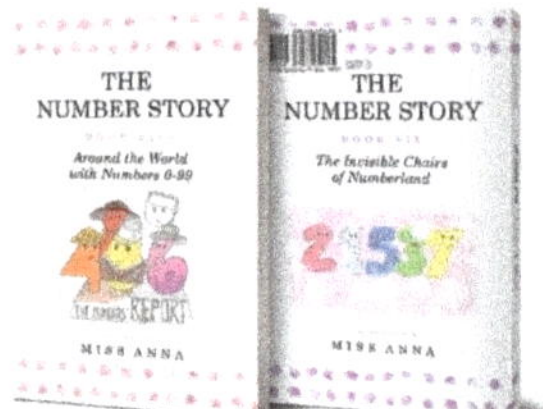

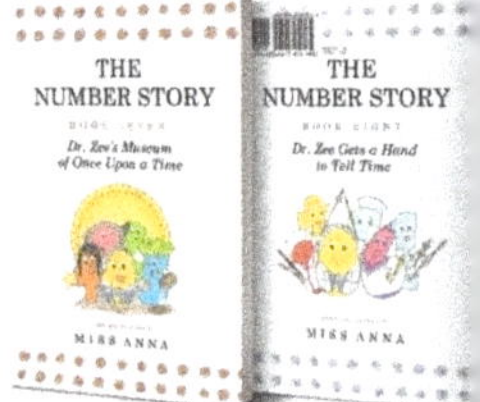

Number Story 1 & 2
isbn: 978-0-996216-48-7

Number Story 3 & 4
isbn: 978-1-945977-01-5

Number Story 5 & 6
isbn: 978-1-945977-06-0

Number Story 7 & 8
isbn: 978-1-949320-40-

For more Miss Anna books to love,
visit us at

www.missannabooks.com

Numbers are working hard all over the world!
Come Travel the World with Us!

9 781945 977404